OH,
The
AUDACITY
TALES!
Tara Ijai &
Deedra Abboud

Disclaimer and Terms of Use:

The Author and Publisher has strived to be as accurate and complete as possible in the creation of this book, notwithstanding the fact that she does not warrant or represent at any time that the contents within are accurate due to the rapidly changing nature of the Internet. While all attempts have been made to verify information provided in this publication, the Author and Publisher assume no responsibility for errors, omissions, or contrary interpretation of the subject matter herein. Any perceived slights of specific persons, peoples, or organizations are unintentional.

ISBN ISBN: 978-1-956565-36-2

This book is dedicated to:

**Love Rebels
on a journey of personal
discovery and growth.**

May embracing your true self bring you joy!

***In the bustling office
where the air was always buzzing
with activity and loads of paper,
there was one person who stood out
amongst the crowd.***

***Her name was Tara,
and she was known for her
quirky humor and playful antics.***

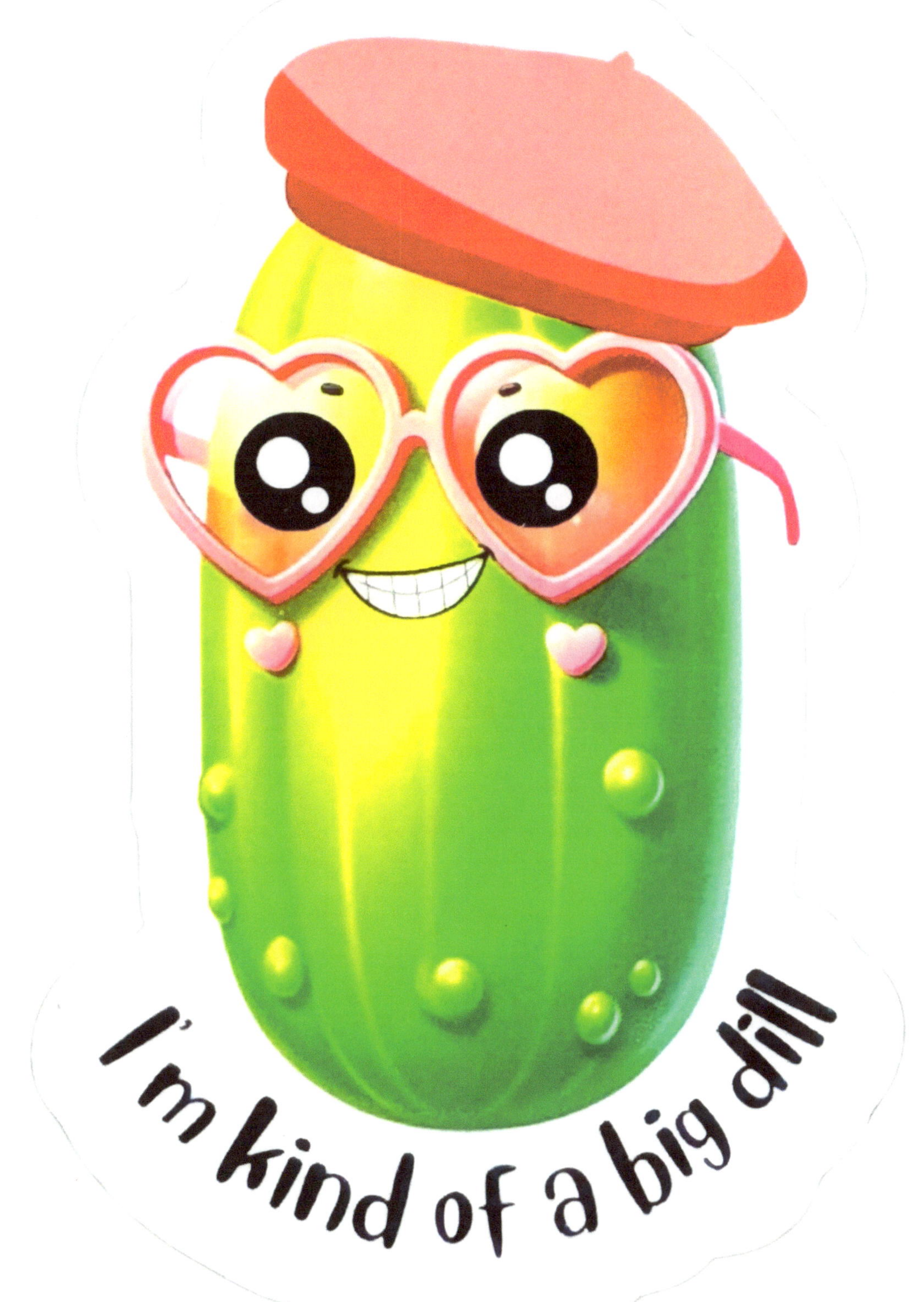
I'm kind of a big dill

***But more than that,
Tara had a special talent for creating whimsical stickers that captured feelings, emotions, and idioms in the most colorful and imaginative way possible.***

It was an obsession really.

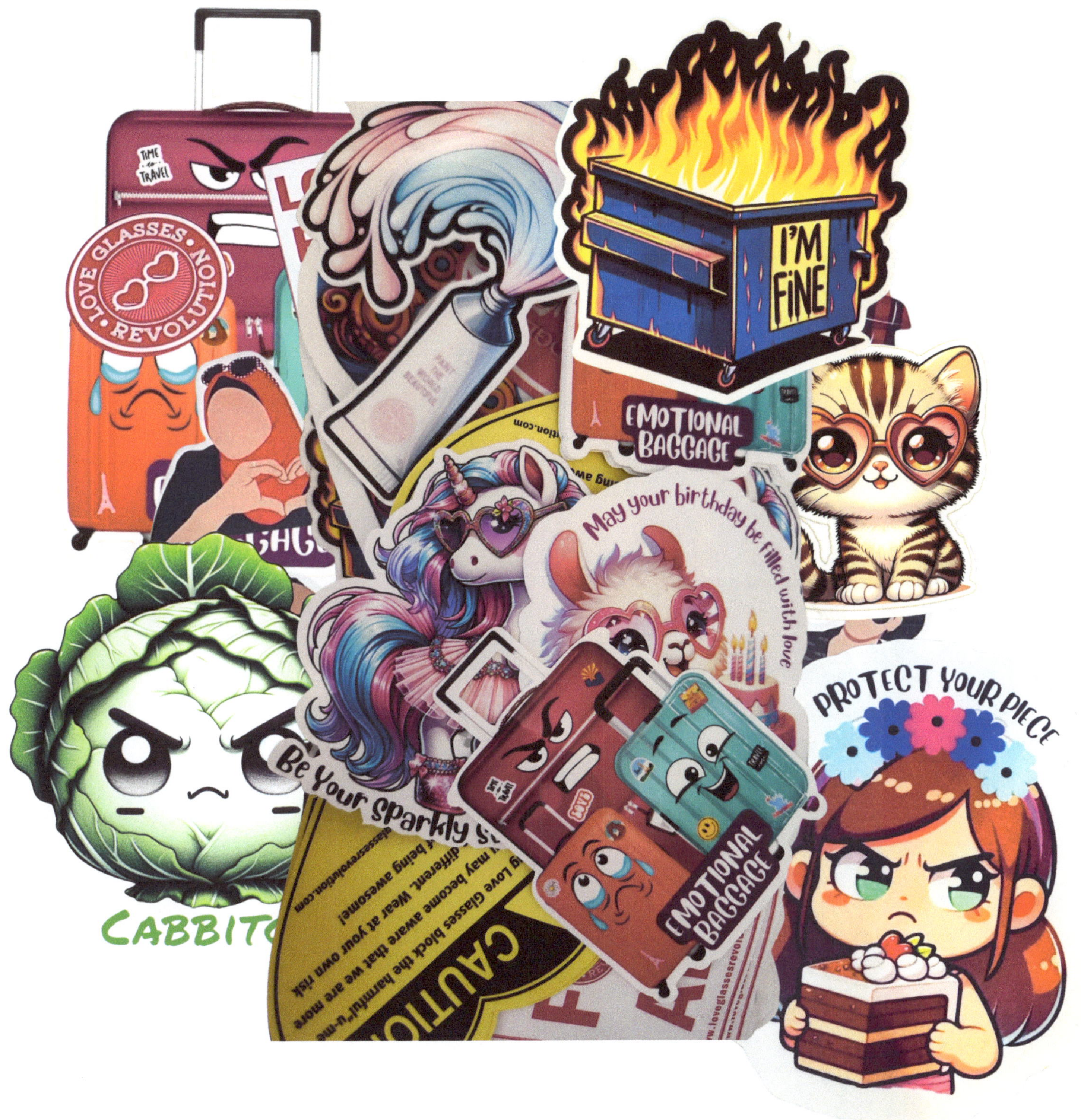
TIME to TRAVEL
LOVE GLASSES REVOLUTION
I'M FINE
EMOTIONAL BAGGAGE
May your birthday be filled with love
PROTECT YOUR PIECE
Be Your sparkly
EMOTIONAL BAGGAGE
CAUTION

One legendary moment
in our office stands out,
a moment that truly showcased
the power of Tara's stickers
to uplift and unite us all.

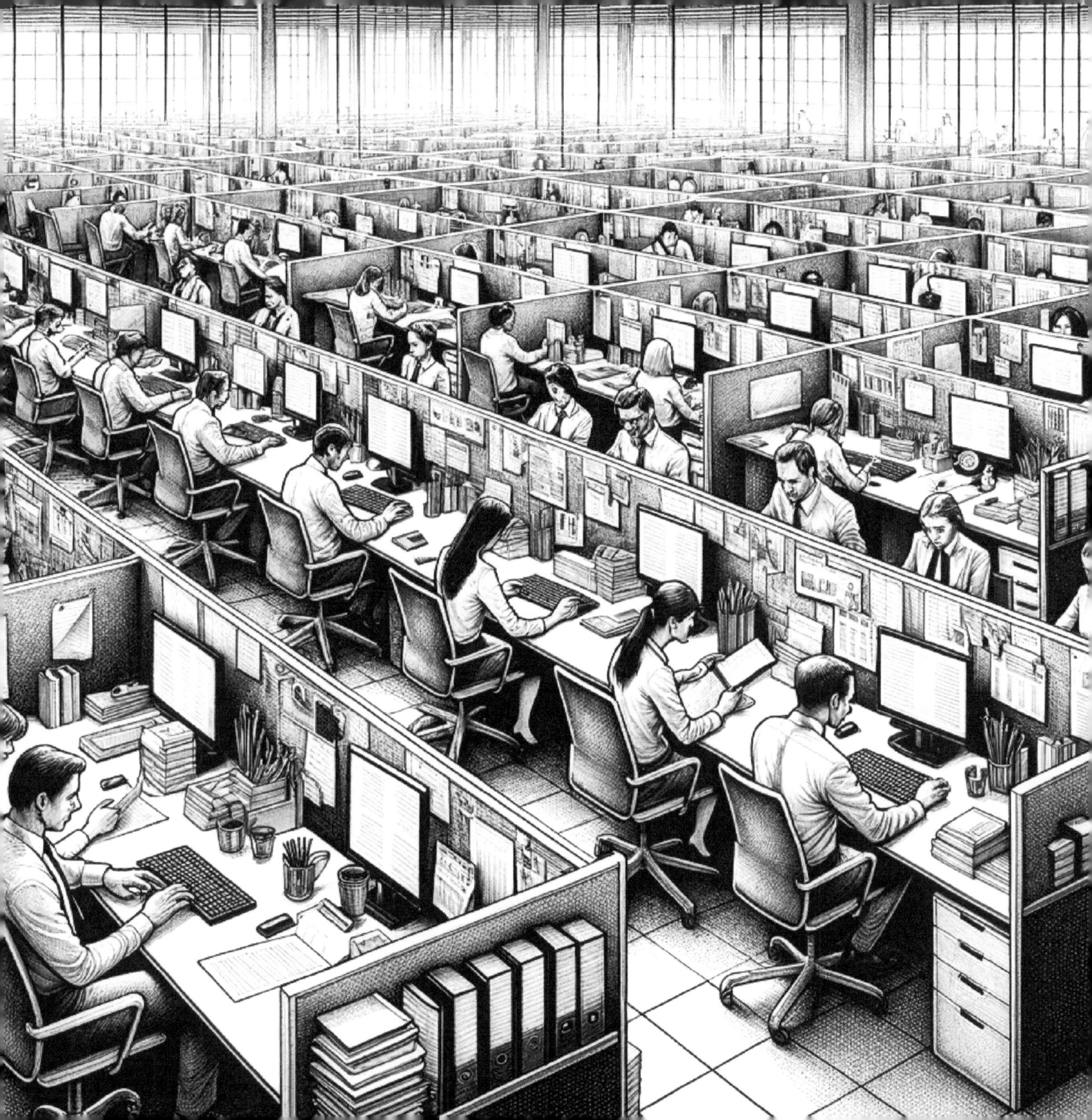

It all started when a visitor graced our office with her presence, regaling our office manager with a captivating story.

But it was her exclamation of "Can you believe the AUDACITY?" that sparked something magical in the air.

Can you believe the Audacity?!

It was like a bat signal for Tara,
who knew she had just the sticker
for this moment.

With a rush of excitement,
she reached for the perfect sticker in
her sticker stash,
only to realize she had given away
her last one earlier that day.

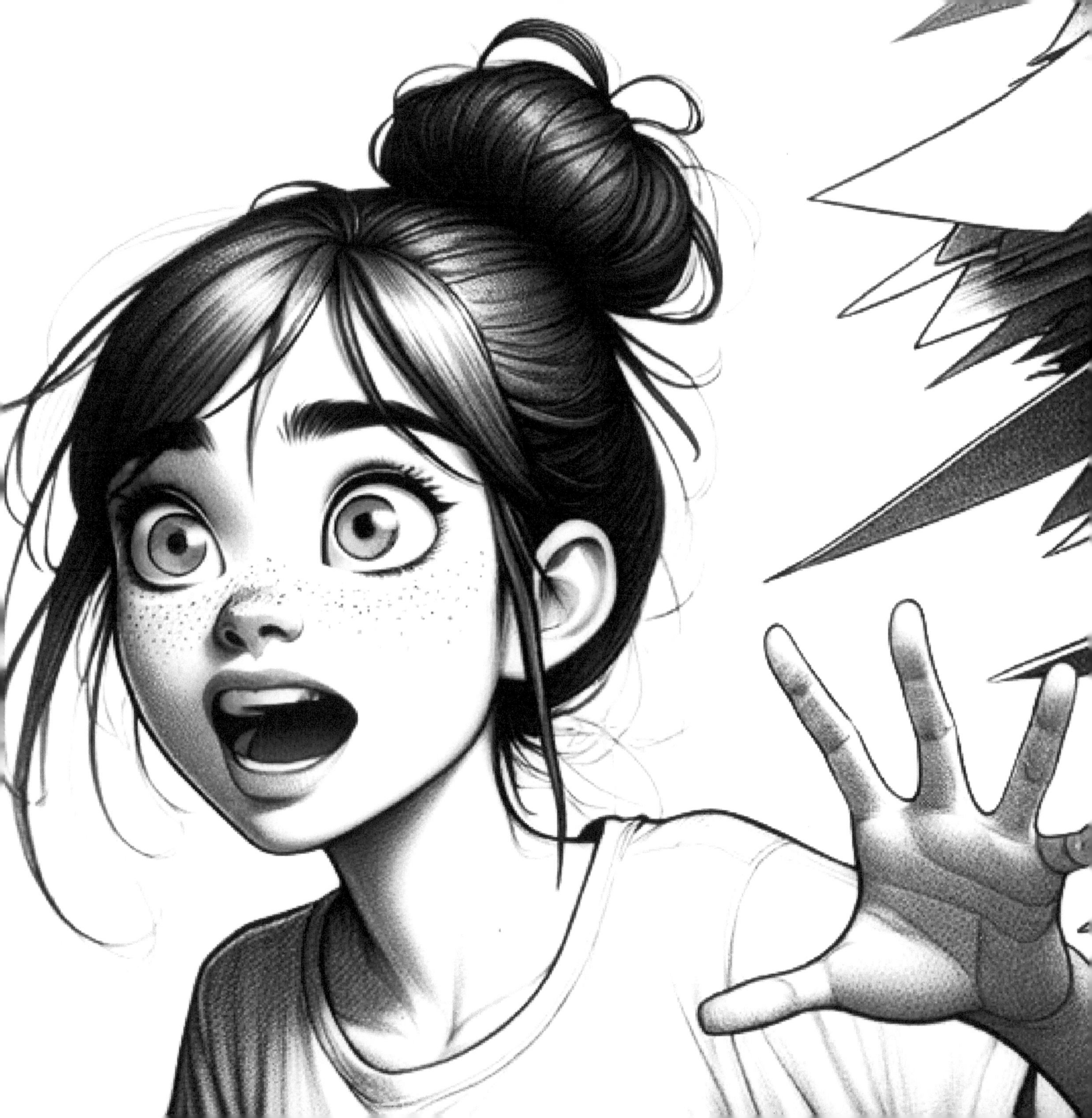

In almost the same instant,
a hand pops up from the next cubicle
and we hear a chirp of,
"Here, take it!"

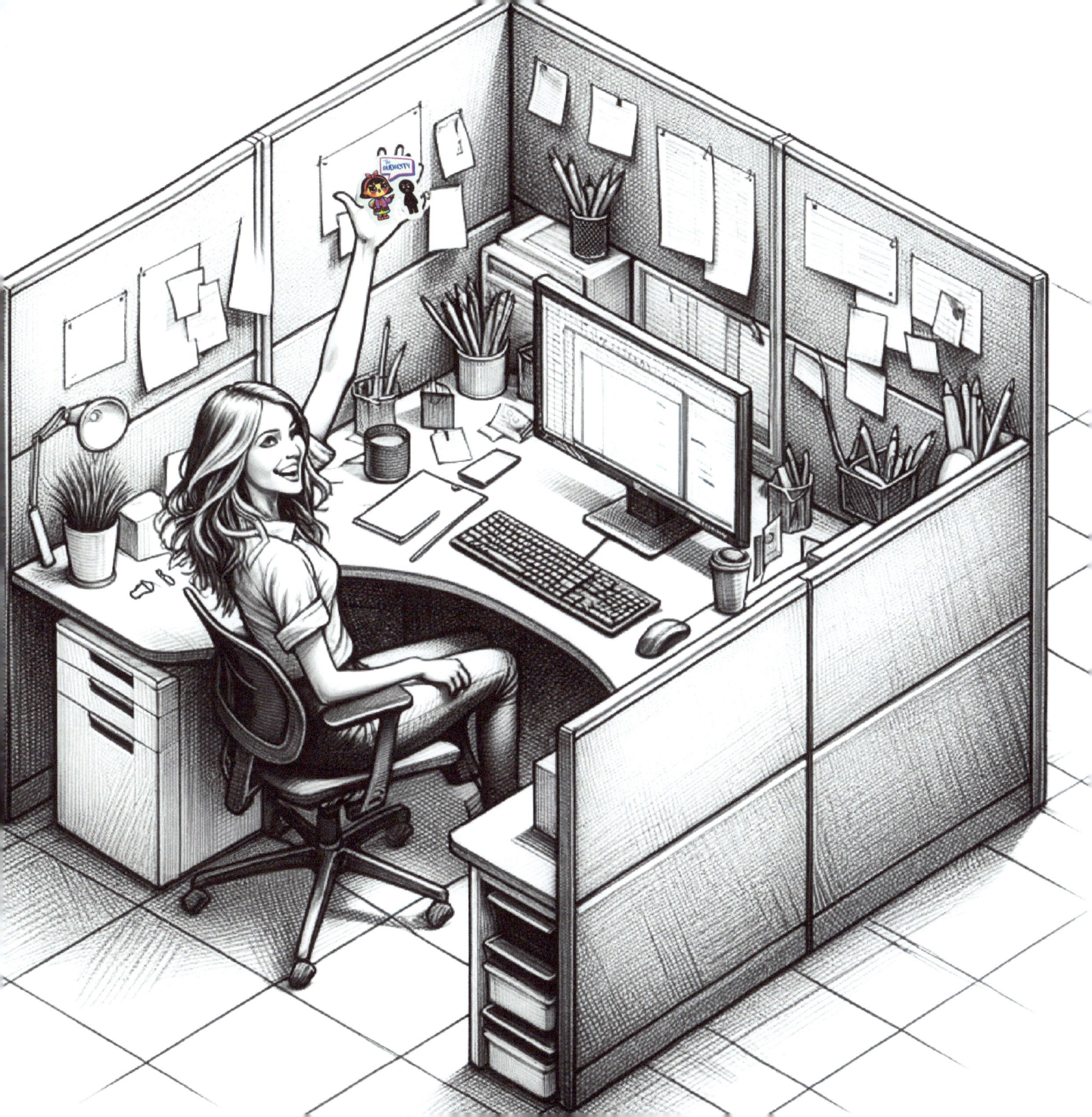
The AUDACITY

Tara's eyes well up with tears,
her heart overflowing with gratitude
for her co-worker's quick wit and
unwavering support.

Her heart pounding
with anticipation,
she seizes the sticker
like a relay baton,
already mid-sprint
toward the office manager's door.

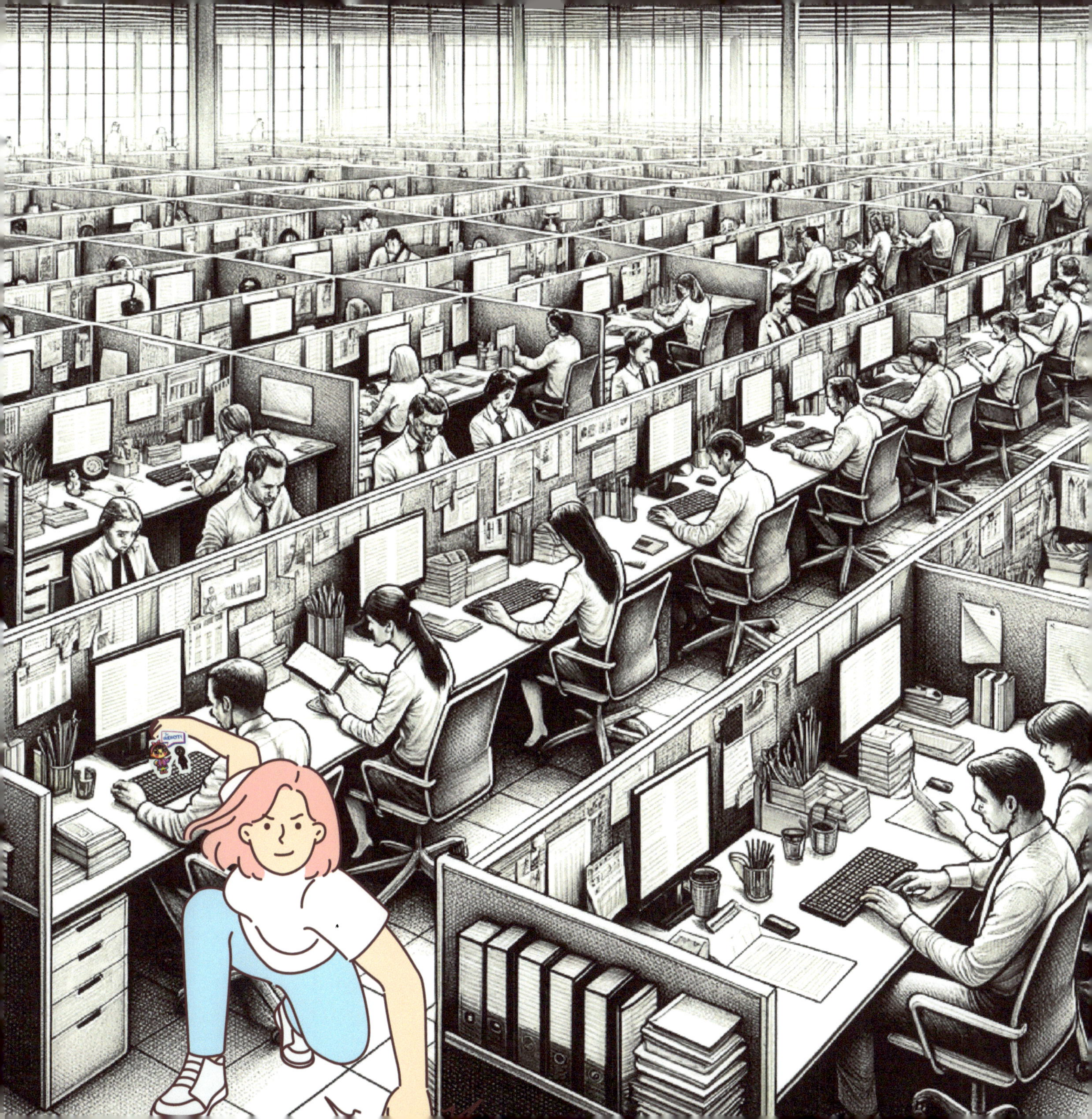

Rounding the corner
faster than any
major leaguer rounding bases
(pretty sure),
Tara's smile waned
faster than her heavy panting...

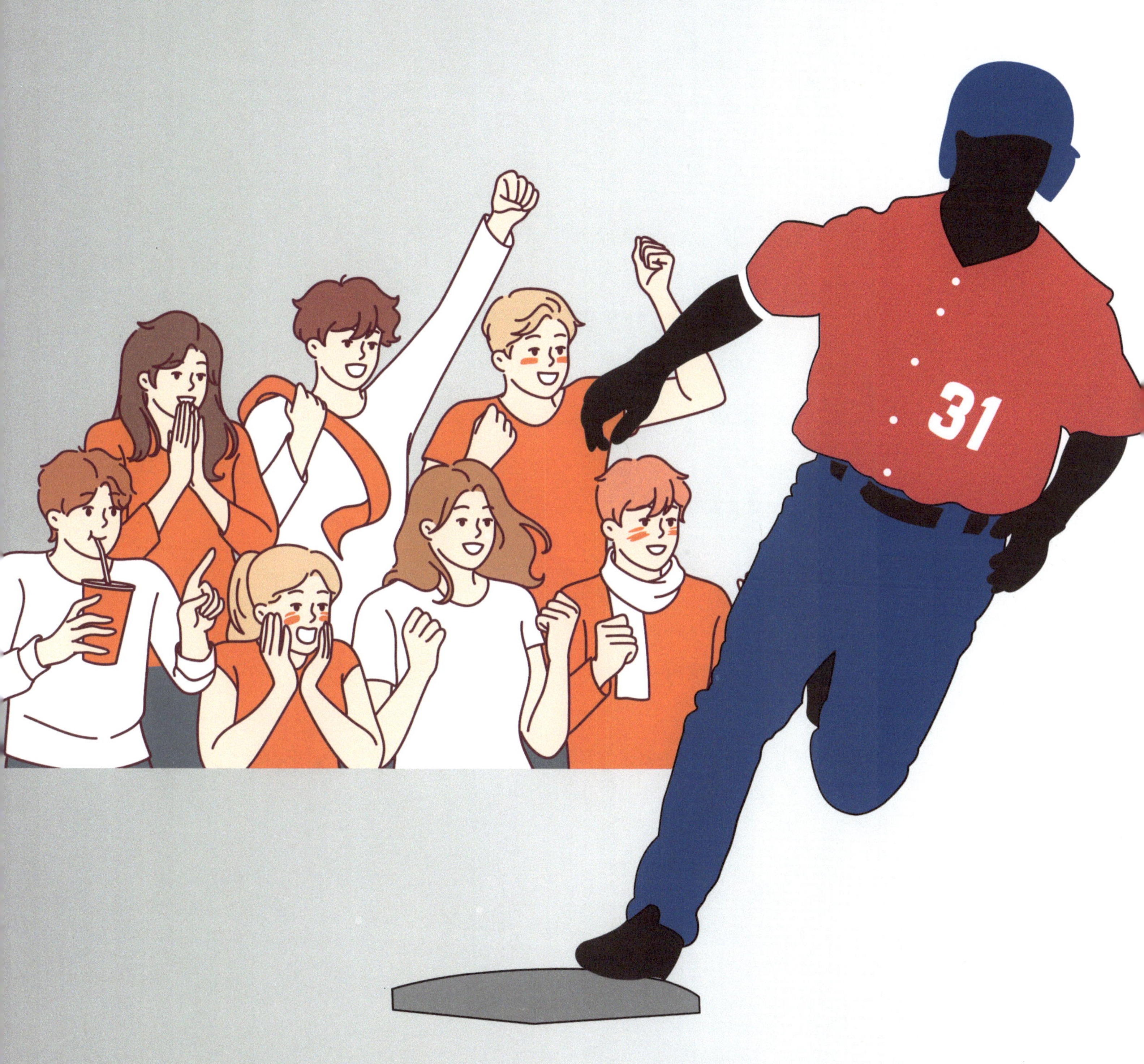
31

Because alas,
she was just a hair too late,
as the office manager
had already presented
the visitor with the
very same perfect sticker.

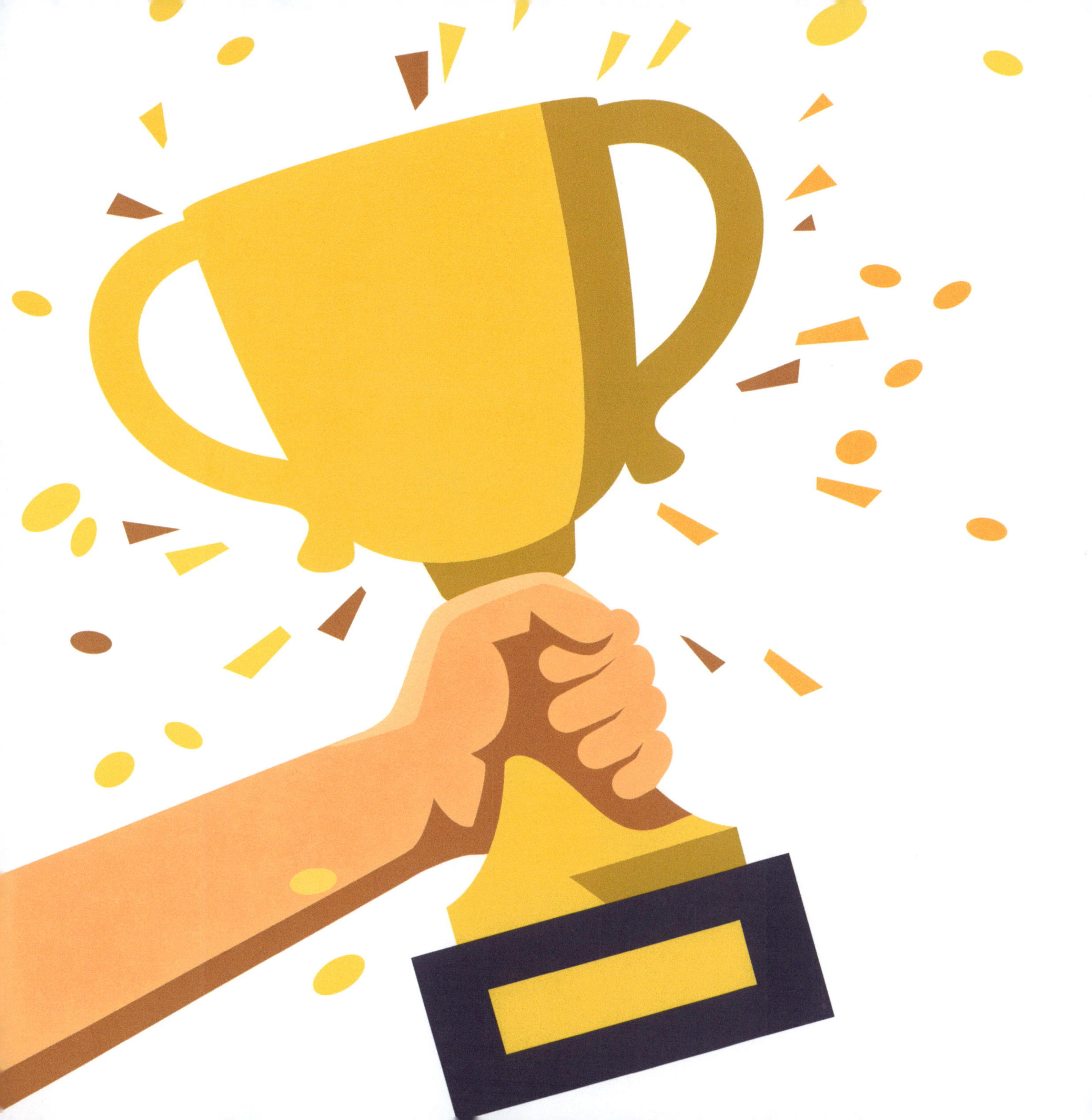

But the visitor didn't miss a beat
as she saw Tara's arm
slide through the
open doorway showing
"The Audacity!"

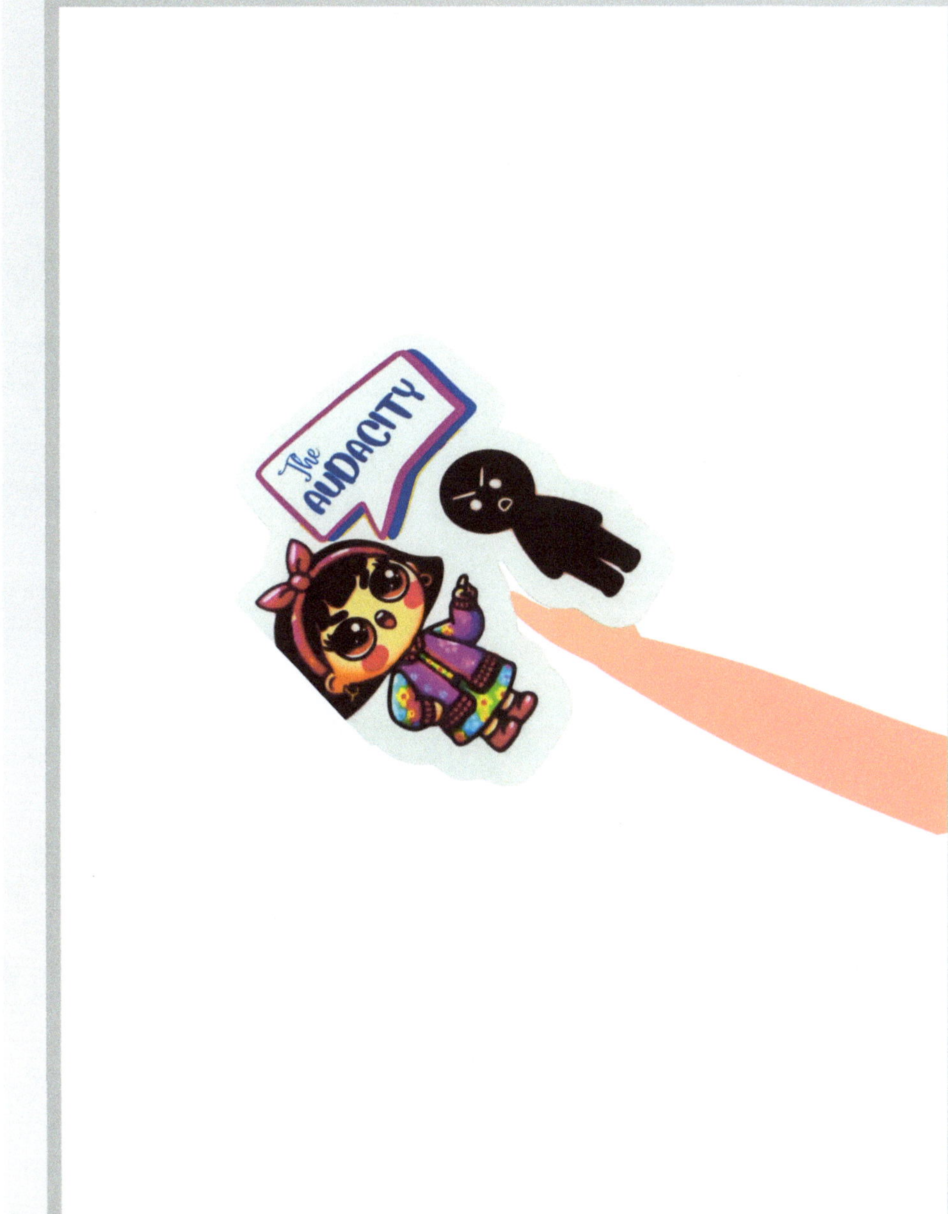
The AUDACITY

With pure joy and excitement,
the visitor exclaimed
how thrilled she was to have
not one, but two
of Tara's stickers—
—one for her laptop
and one for her water bottle.

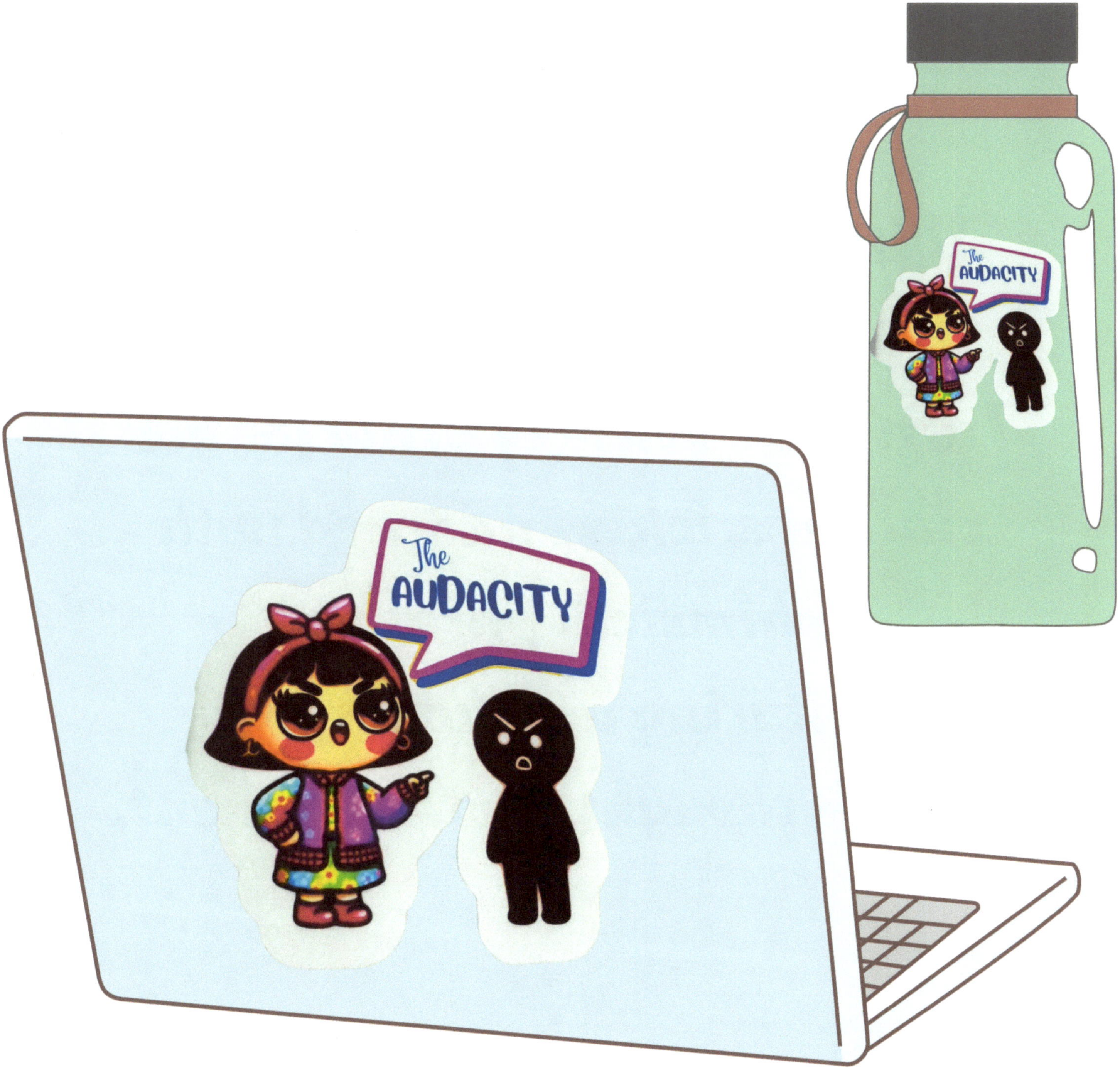

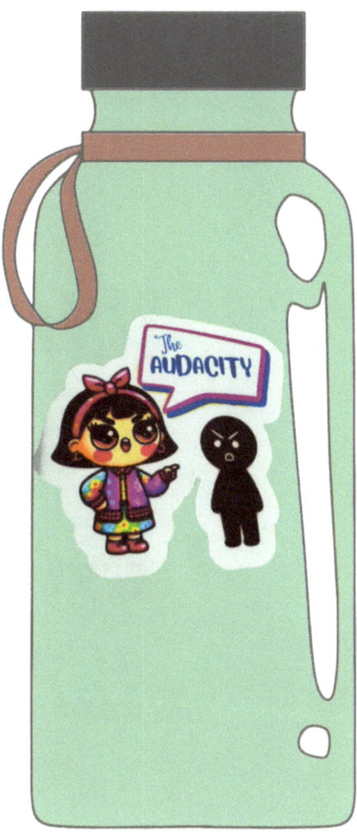
The AUDACITY

With her smile now beaming
brighter than ever,
Tara felt a sense of pride for her
vibrant stickers adorned with
whimsical phrases,
capturing and honoring
people's thoughts in the moment.

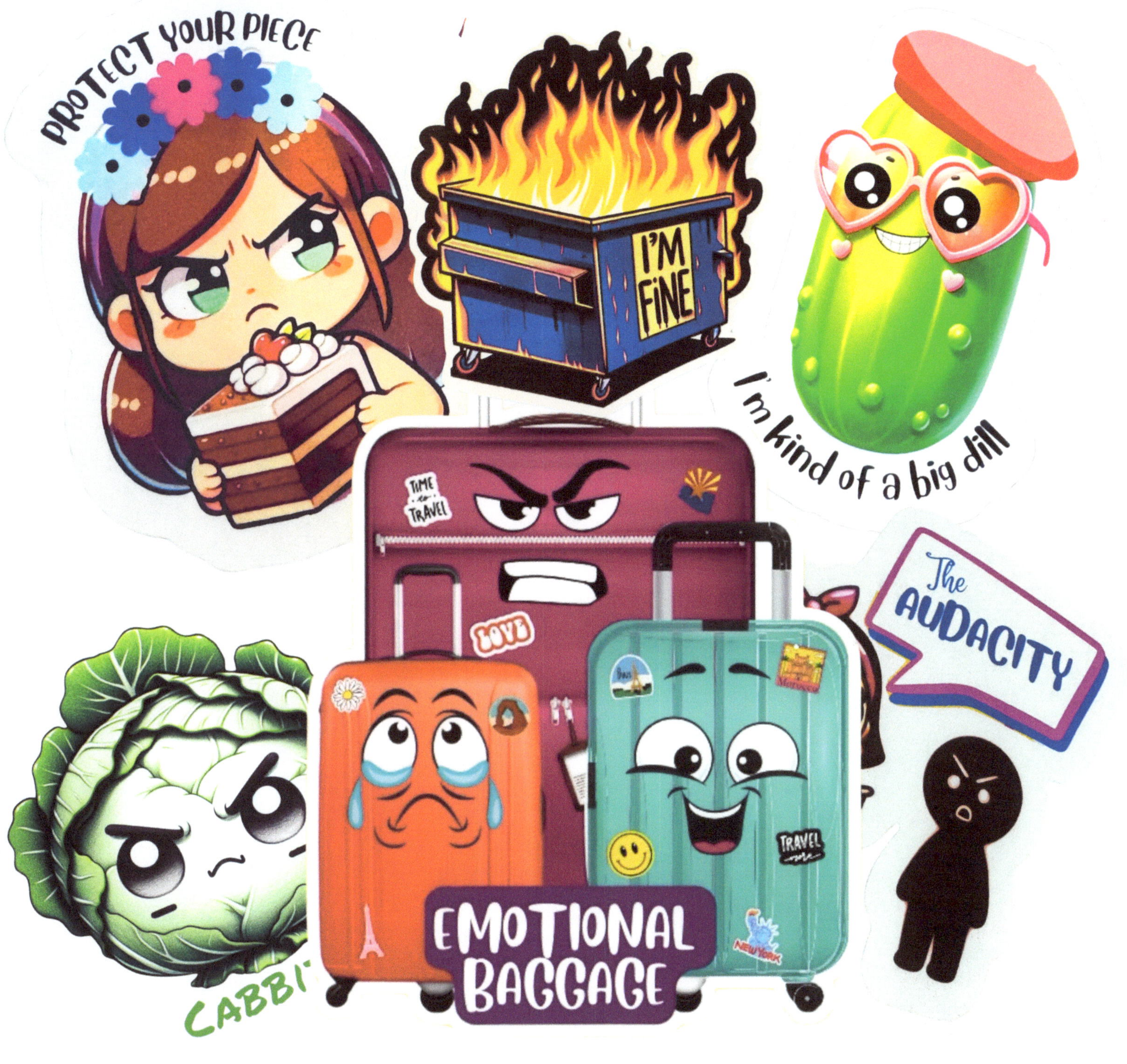
PROTECT YOUR PIECE
I'M FINE
I'm kind of a big dill
TIME to TRAVEL
LOVE
The AUDACITY
TRAVEL
NEW YORK
EMOTIONAL BAGGAGE

We heard the Audacity,
we knew the audacity,
and we were the audacity!

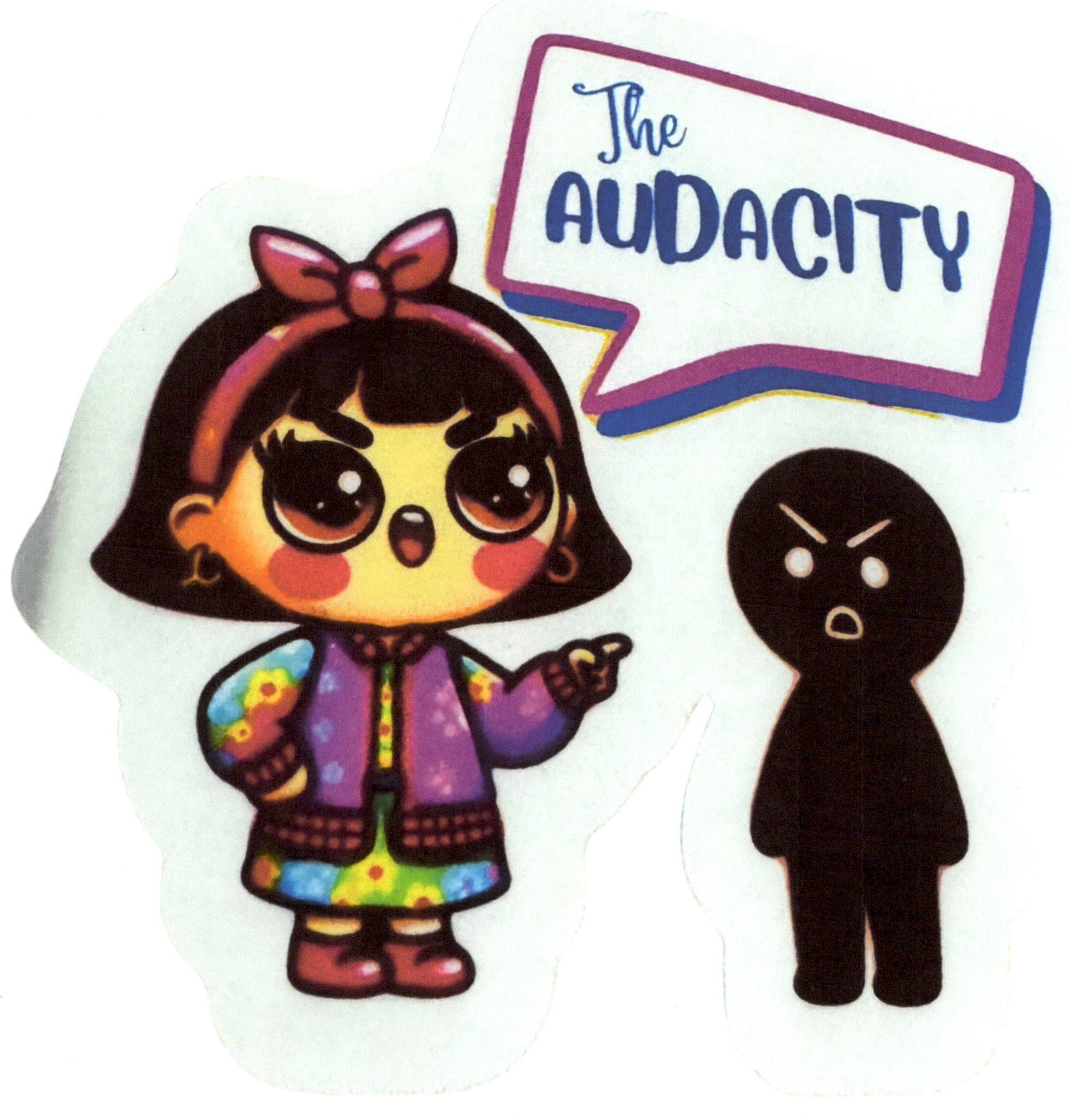
The AUDACITY

*In that moment,
Tara realized something incredible:
her stickers were more than just
colorful pieces of adhesive—
—they were symbols of
connection and joy,
spreading happiness
wherever they went.*

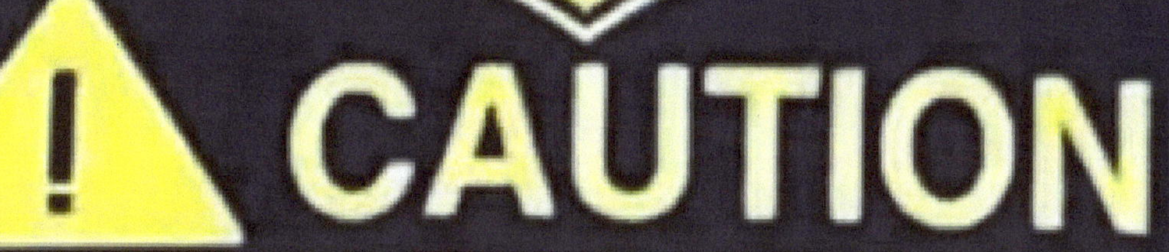

Wearing Love Glasses block the harmful"u-me" rays. You may become aware that we are more alike than different. Wear at your own risk of being awesome!

www.loveglassesrevolution.com

As we all shared in the laughter and camaraderie that followed, Tara knew that her stickers had the power to make a difference, to bring people together in unexpected ways.

LOVE

F R

ALL

LOVE GLASSES REVOLUTION

www.loveglassesrevolution.com

Tara's eyes spanned the office,
from the joyful face of the visitor
to the victorious office manager
to her excited cubicled co-workers,
and knew her work here was done...

well, not her actual work

but well...

you know what I'm saying.

And so, armed with her trusty
stickers and her endless creativity,
Tara continues to spread joy,
one sticker at a time,
reminding us all to embrace
who we are and to share
our unique gifts with the world.

Check out Tara's sticker collection:

@LoveGlassesRevolution

www.ingramcontent.com/pod-product-compliance
Lightning Source LLC
LaVergne TN
LVHW070223110826
845147LV00003B/633

9781956565362